WE

STILL BELIEVE

2025

By: Samuel Leonard

Dedication

I would like to dedicate this book to my wife, Kinsey Leonard, and our three children: Gabriel, Caroline, and Priscilla. You are my joy, the Lord's greatest gifts to me. Without my wife's patience, encouragement and support this book would not be published. I not only found my Proverbs 31 wife, but the woman with the purest heart of anyone I know. I love you, darling.

Table of Contents

Foreword

Rev. Timothy Nail, Pastor at Lake City Pentecostal Holiness Church

I have known Pastor Samuel Leonard since he was a young college student at Holmes Bible College. Pastor Sam has been one of the greatest defenders of the Pentecostal Faith I have ever known. God has gifted him with an amazing mind, and he has used that mind to study God's Word. His great education has not detoured him from his faith, or his Pentecostal upbringing. Like other great educated men like Dr. Ray H. Hughes, Pastor Sam has a true experience with the Holy Ghost that cannot be trumped by man's wisdom. In this book, Pastor Sam brings not the enticing words of man's wisdom but the power and demonstration of the Holy Ghost by taking a methodical look into the New Testament Scriptures concerning the physical, initial evidence of Spirit baptism just as the students in Topeka, Kansas did nearly 125 years ago. He then lays out for the reader the Biblical understanding of why the Classical Pentecostal Movement stands so firm on the doctrine of speaking in tongues as the initial evidence of the Baptism of the Holy Ghost.

We Still Believe

And when the day of Pentecost was fully come, they were all with one accord in one place. [2] And suddenly there came a sound from Heaven as of a rushing mighty wind, and it filled all the house where they were sitting. [3] And there appeared unto them cloven tongues like as of fire, and it sat upon each of them. [4] And they were all filled with the Holy Ghost, and began to speak with other tongues, as the Spirit gave them utterance ***(Acts 2:1-4)***.

It has been nearly 2,000 years since the 120 Jews had their personal Pentecost, and as they did, there are still many receiving this promise of power today. However, as experienced in the early church, Pentecost has come underneath attack. The Jews that were filled with the Holy Ghost Baptism were accused of being drunk ***(c.f. Acts 2:12-13)***, but this was most assuredly not the case. Around 700 years before Christ's promise of power to the disciples, Isaiah prophesied: *"For with stammering lips and another tongue will He speak to this people. [12] To whom He said, This is the rest wherewith ye may cause the weary to rest; and this is the refreshing: yet they would not hear"* ***(Isa. 28:11-12)***. The apostle Paul, while speaking to the Corinthian church about the use of prophecy and tongues, quotes Isaiah ***(c.f. 1 Cor. 14:21-22)***. Tongues were used as a sign to the unbelievers in this instance; however, tongues are not merely used as a sign to sinners but edification for the saints. Why would God, out of everything, use tongues as a sign that one has been baptized in the Spirit? I believe that James gives clarity to this, *"But the tongue can no man tame"* ***(Jam. 3:8)***. The man of wisdom, Solomon, penned these words, *"Death and life are in the power of the tongue: and they that love it shall eat the fruit thereof"* ***(Prov. 18:21)***. Whenever one is baptized in the Holy Ghost, it is total submission to God. The hardest member of the body to tame, which man has failed to domesticate, has now been subjugated by the authority of Heaven.

Today, in most current Pentecostal churches, a shift has taken place where there is an absence of the tangible anointing of God. Before one criticizes this statement, let me address this "issue." I know what some may be thinking, "God is omnipresent, His anointing is everywhere." No, this is not the case. God is omnipresent, everywhere, but His tangible anointing does not rest on every house. David declared, *"If I ascend up into Heaven, Thou art there: if I make my bed in Hell, behold, Thou art there"* ***(Ps. 139:8)***. Though God is everywhere, there is an absence of His love and grace in Hell ***(c.f. Matt. 25:41)***. A patriarch of the faith, Moses, knew that God's tangible anointing needed to go with he and the Israelites if they were to ever be successful in possessing their promise. He said, *"If Thy presence go not with me, carry us not up hence"* ***(Ex. 33:15)***. The man who was lowered into the house where Jesus abided went for a purpose, *"...the power of the Lord was present to heal them"* ***(Lk. 5:17)***. Examples are made throughout the Scriptures such as God's *shekinah* glory filling Solomon's Temple ***(2 Chron. 7:1-3)***; the anointing resting on God's choice servants such as Peter that while walking his shadow touched the diseased and demonized, delivering them ***(Acts 5:15-16)***. The tangible presence of God can either be received or rejected ***(c.f. Judg. 16:20)***. Sadly, we have focused on education, entertainment, and manmade ingenuity rather than the promised empowerment. We have created an atmosphere to attract people rather than the presence of God. People are worshiping a God that they do not know ***(c.f. Acts 10:1-2)***. What has changed? Our perspective. Within the next few pages, I hope to answer questions and bring clarity to the Baptism of the Holy Ghost, leaving the reader declaring, "We still believe!"

Chapter 1

God's Covenant

God is not a man, that He should lie; neither the son of man, that He should repent: hath He said, and shall He not do it? or hath He spoken, and shall He not make it good ***(Num. 23:19)****.*

Most scholars would agree that the Lord is a covenant God. Found throughout the Bible, His covenants can be combined into seven categories: the Adamic ***(Gen. 1:26-2:3)***, Noahic ***(Gen. 9:8-17)***, Abrahamic ***(Gen. 12:1-3; 17:1-14)***, Mosaic ***(Exod. 19:5-6)***, Davidic ***(2 Sam. 7:18-19)***, New ***(Jer. 31:31-34; Matt. 5:17; Eph. 2:8-9)***, and Everlasting ***(Eph. 3:11-12; Rom. 8:28-30)*** covenants. Though this is the list of Seven Major Covenants, this cannot summarize all that God has coveted with His people. The word "covenant" appears for the first time in ***Genesis 6:18*** and occurs 270 other times in the Old Testament alone. In the entirety of the Bible, there are well over 7,400 promises God has made, and not one of them has He failed at fulfilling; devils nor doubters can dissolve what God has declared. Every covenant that has been instituted by God has and will come to fruition.

Concerning the Spirit Baptism, this covenant was made accessible after Christ's ascension. As our Lord prepared for His ascension to Heaven, He admonished His disciples to follow His directive: *"And, behold, I send the promise of My Father upon you: but tarry ye in the city of Jerusalem, until you be endued with power from on high"* ***(Lk. 24:49)***. In the New Testament, the covenant not only guaranteed salvation through the blood but power from the Spirit Baptism. The disciples were not to desert nor drift, but DWELL until they had been clothed in anointing. Dr. Frank Tunstall writes, "Then Jesus introduced the disciples to what would be required for them to become His sent ones. He breathed on them and said, 'Receive the Holy Spirit' ***(John 20:22)***. The term, *breathed*, comes from *emphusao*, and it communicates to *puff* or *blow* on them. The implication here is that the Holy Spirit was the breath of God that the Lord delighted to breathe into His thirsty followers a few weeks up the road." Before the disciples could be sent, they had to be filled.

Luke continues to pen the record of Christ, consisting

of His miracles and mandates, then transitions to the book of *Acts.* Writing to Theopolis, Luke cites another one of Jesus' remarks concerning the promised Comforter, *"But ye shall receive power, after that the Holy Ghost is come upon you: and ye shall be witnesses unto Me both in Jerusalem, and in all Judaea, and in Samaria, and unto the uttermost part of the earth"* ***(Acts 1:8)***. This power, as will be discussed, has not been disjoined from believers.

After Jesus ascended to Heaven, His disciples entered the upper room and began praying and seeking this blessed promise. Ten days passed when Heaven's Holy Ghost filled these men and women, approximately 120, and they went into the streets speaking in other tongues, declaring the wonderful works of God. Now, I know that skeptics will use this specific passage to criticize modern day believers who speak in tongues, declaring that what is done today is nothing more than "gibberish." Their case may possibly have a basis if it was not for various Scriptures and patterns; this was not the only occurrence nor the only usage of glossolalia in the New Testament Church. Tongues are used in three ways: evidence, edification, and exhalation.

- **Tongues as Initial Evidence**- The first recorded

instance that speaking in tongues occurred is ***Acts 2***, but this was not the only time that it happened. ***Acts 8***, the Samaritans believed on Christ and were baptized. Here, they were converted but there was something missing, the Holy Ghost Baptism. Scripture records, *"Now when the apostles which were at Jerusalem heard that Samaria had received the Word of God, they sent unto them Peter and John: [15] Who, when they were come down, prayed for them, that they might receive the Holy Ghost: [16] (For as yet He was fallen upon none of them: only they were baptized in the Name of the Lord Jesus)"* ***(Acts 8:14-16)***. Though tongues were not specifically identified, there was evidence the Samaritans received the Holy Ghost insomuch that Simon the Sorcerer wanted to purchase the power Peter and John prayed for them to have. Bishop A. D. Beacham, Jr. states that, "although tongues are not specifically mentioned, <u>some physical manifestation occurred</u> because Simon saw evidence that when the apostles laid hands on the people, they received the Spirit." It is here, in ***Acts 8***, where "the strongest evidence for a subsequent experience of the Spirit" occurred. "The Samaritans obviously experienced conversion when

Philip preached Christ, resulting in joy in the city ***(Acts 8:4, 8)***. Verse twelve emphatically states that the Samaritans believed and were baptized in response to their faith. Sometime afterward, Peter and John prayed for them to receive the Holy Spirit ***(Acts 8:17)***." By examining the passage Scripturally and logically, when one believes on the Lord Jesus Christ they are saved, and the Holy Spirit lives within them ***(Eph. 1:13-14; 1 Cor. 3:16; Rom. 8:9)***. If this is the case, then why were Peter and John sent? The answer is simple, there is a subsequent work for the believer, the Holy Ghost Baptism.

Next, in ***Acts 9***, Paul was on the road to Damascus whenever he had an encounter with the risen Christ. He was told to enter the city and find a man by the name of Ananias. Ananias, not even an apostle as some skeptics claim you had to be to perform miracles and impart the Spirit Baptism, prayed over Paul where he received not only his sight but the Holy Ghost ***(Acts 9:17)***. Did Paul speak in tongues? Some say he did not here because it was not recorded, but whenever Paul wrote to the Corinthian church he declared, *"I thank my God, I speak with tongues more than ye all"* ***(1 Cor. 14:18)***. Not only did Paul pray in tongues, but he sang in the Spirit as well ***(1 Cor. 14:15)***. Stanley Horton provides commentary on ***Acts 9:15-18***, "Then Ananias obeyed, entered the house, and laid his hands on Saul, calling him 'brother.' By this he recognized that Saul was now a believer." Ananias said that there were two items on God's agenda, first to remove the scales so Saul could see; next, he was to pray over him that he would receive the Holy Ghost. If Saul was already saved, there would have to be evidence of his reception of the Spirit. "Once again, we see that Luke does not repeat everything in every place. In effect, he indicates that Saul's experience in being filled with the Holy Spirit was no different from that experienced on the Day of Pentecost. We can be sure he spoke in other tongues at that time as they did in ***Acts 2:4***." In ***Titus 3:5-7***, it confirms the Holy Spirit was abundantly poured out upon Paul and Timothy.

The fourth case for tongues as the initial evidence is found in ***Acts 10***. Some scholars say it could have been up to thirty years after Pentecost before Gentile believers were receiving this gift from God. Cornelius, a centurion in the Italian regiment, was a believer in God but did not have the knowledge and understanding about Jesus. God sends Peter to his house to preach the Gospel, and we are told, *"While Peter yet spake these words, the Holy Ghost fell on all them which heard the word. [45] And they of the circumcision which believed were astonished, as many as came with Peter, because that on the gentiles also was poured out the gift of the Holy Ghost. [46] For they heard them speak with tongues, and magnify God" (***Acts 10:44-46***)*. Here, the Bible records that the evidence for them receiving the Holy Ghost was they all spoke in tongues. There are three elements related to the Day of Pentecost and what occurred at Cornelius' house: "(1) the verb describing the manifestation of the Spirit, "poured out" (Gk. *ekcheo*), (2) their speaking with tongues (languages), and (3) those tongues magnifying God…It also shows that the Pentecostal experience can be repeated." If tongues were used as merely a language to witness, why did the Gentiles need this experience because Peter and the Jews were all believers?

Finally, the fifth piece of evidence is found in ***Acts 19***. As Paul encounters the Ephesian believers, they had not yet received the Holy Ghost. In fact, the Bible records they had not even heard that there was a Holy Ghost. Paul lays his hands on them, and this is what happened, *"And when Paul had laid his hands upon them, the Holy Ghost came on them; and they spake with tongues and prophesied"* ***(Acts 19:6)***. About twelve men received the Holy Ghost baptism, and it was evident to Paul whenever they spoke in tongues. As asked in the previous example, "Why would the Ephesians need to speak in a foreign language when Paul was there because he was saved? Speaking in tongues testified that they were endued with Heavenly power.

- **Tongues as Edification-** In ***1 Corinthians 12***, Paul listed 9 manifestation gifts of the Spirit. Manifestation gifts are active whenever the church is gathered as a corporate body. *"But the <u>manifestation</u> of the Spirit is given to every man to profit withal"* ***(1 Cor. 12:7)***. As the Spirit of God would come upon individuals, they would speak in an unknown tongue to the church which then required an interpretation to bring about edification to the body of believers. Paul's desire was for the whole church to speak in tongues, but the greatest gift in a corporate setting was prophecy unless there was an interpreter present to decipher the message in tongues, which would then bring spiritual benefits to all believers ***(1 Cor. 14:3-5)***. It should also be noted that the Greek word rendered "interpret" does not always mean "translate;" there is ample evidence that the word also means "explain." As in ***Luke 24:27,*** it states that Christ expounded to the disciples all the scriptures concerning himself. The same Greek word was used for "interpret" and "expounded." Behm states in *Theological Dictionary of the New Testament*, "The Interpretation of tongues can hardly be a translation; it is a conversion of what is unintelligible into what is intelligible."

The Corinthian church was chaotic, multiple people giving messages in tongues without interpretation, bringing not only disruption but confusion. Paul brought correction, *"If any man speak in an unknown tongue, let it be by two, or at the most by three, and that by course; and let one interpret"* ***(1 Cor. 14:27)***. The manifestation gift of speaking in tongues would bring about necessary spiritual strength to the local assembly, which is why we are not to forbid speaking in tongues ***(1 Cor. 14:39)***.

- **Tongues as Exaltation-** Praying in the Spirit is not new terminology, but it has come underneath attack by some believing it is "gibberish;" yet this is not what the apostle Paul believed. *"For if I pray in an unknown tongue, my spirit prayeth"* ***(1 Cor. 14:14)***. The one who speaks in tongues edifies themselves ***(1 Cor. 14:4)***, and it builds up our spiritual man/woman. This is not the only place where Paul references praying in the Spirit, in fact he speaks to the church at Rome and Ephesus and says, *"Likewise the Spirit also helpeth our infirmities: for we know not what we should pray for as we ought: but the Spirit itself maketh intercession for us with groanings which cannot be uttered. [27] And He that searcheth the hearts knoweth what is the mind of the Spirit, because He maketh intercession for the saints according to the will of God"* ***(Rom. 8:26-27)***; *"Praying always with all prayer and supplication in the Spirit"* ***(Eph. 6:18)***. Furthermore, Jude writes, *"But ye, beloved, building up yourselves on your* *most holy faith, praying in the Holy Ghost"* ***(Jude 20).*** Praying in the Spirit is not a foreign concept, but it has been abandoned by many Pentecostal churches. God does not wish for anyone's spirit to be depleted which is why He gave us access to the anointing, by praying in the Spirit.

Testimony: My wife, Kinsey, and I pastored our first church in 2018. This small community, Neeses, had a population of about 400 people. God began blessing this church and nearly 200 people would attend services on any given Sunday morning. Shortly after, the dreaded Covid-19 virus struck, our church conducted services outside. April 13th, 2020, an event occurred that would forever change this little community. Around 5:30 AM, two F-3 tornadoes touched down and devastated our community and surrounding areas. Two people in our area passed with many hospitalized and others left homeless. Our church sprang into action, feeding the community and power companies for nearly two weeks. Churches from all over donated money as we were gifting the families affected with a small monetary gift. As we were winding down with the community effort, a lady came to the parsonage and said, "Pastor, can I speak with you?"

This conversation would forever change my life. As we talked, she said, "Pastor, I am Baptist." I responded that we did not care what denomination, we were more than happy to assist her. She said, "No Pastor, you do not understand, I am Baptist." Again, I interrupted her and told her that denominations did not matter, we were to show love one to another, and our church was going to bless them. I could tell she was growing frustrated, truthfully, I was a little aggravated myself. I just wanted to give her the offering raised and here she is wanting to talk about denominations. Finally, the third time, she said, "Pastor, I need to tell you something so let me finish. I am Baptist, but something has happened."

She looked at me, with tears in her eyes, and told me of a story I pray I will never forget. "Pastor, the morning the two tornadoes came, my children and I were in my trailer." She and her family lived on Preserver Road, and this was the road with the most damage, leaving two dead, many injured, and about 15 homes damaged and destroyed. As I realized where she was specifically, I listened even more intently. "We heard the alerts, but there was no time for us to go anywhere. We hunkered down in my kitchen, and the trailer lifted from the ground. As we were in the air, I cried out to God, and I began praying but this time was different. I was praying in tongues, a language I did not know nor understand. IMMEDIATELY the trailer sat back down without major damage, and I continued to pray in tongues for forty-five minutes." She wept telling me about her experience. Next, she said, "I was raised Baptist all my life, and I was told that speaking in tongues was demonic. Pastor, I have never experienced this but whenever the tornado came, all I could do was cry out to God, and His Spirit came over me. But Pastor, I am Baptist and do not know what to do." My response to her was simple, "You may be Baptist in name, but you sister, had a Pentecostal experience!"

I know that many will not receive this, but I firmly believe that God is truly desiring to meet with this generation, old and young, giving them an encounter with Him like they have never known. My spiritual father, Pastor Timothy Nail, said something so powerful that he heard from Leonard Ravenhill: "A man with an experience from God is never at the mercy of a man with an argument."

Chapter 2

Skeptics' Challenge

But if any man be ignorant, let him be ignorant ***(1 Cor. 14:38).***

Some will not adhere to sound doctrine due to their preconceived notions or tradition, but the Holy Ghost is a gentleman and will not abide where He is grieved nor commune with those who oppose Him. Paul said to let those who reject the gifts be ignorant, and our responsibility is not to argue but admonish. I find myself, at times, arguing over the case for Pentecost. I have learned; however, pearls should not be cast before swine. There are two major camps that disregard or restrict tongues: cessationists and those who believe that tongues can only be spoken if there is an interpreter present. Here, we will address the first, cessationism.

- **Cessationists**- Cessationists believe that the gifts of the Spirit have been relinquished; that they only happened at the hands of the apostles and early church. Somehow, somewhere, the gifts ceased. This is a far reach for any true believer because the Scriptures do not support this theological assertion.

a. **Argument One-** Miracles were divided into three periods: Moses, Elijah/Elisha, and Jesus and the apostles.

b. **Argument Two-** Miracles waned as the apostles neared the end of their lives; only ***1 Corinthians*** deals with the spiritual gifts and later epistles omit it, meaning they must have ceased.

c. **Argument Three-** Miracles began decreasing as Paul could not heal Timothy ***(1 Tim. 5:23),*** Epaphroditus ***(Philip. 2:25-27)***, or himself ***(2 Cor. 12:9)***.

d. **Argument Four-** Miracles were only used to substantiate the Gospel.

e. **Argument Five-** Tongues were used to evangelize in foreign languages.

f. **Argument Six-** Tongues and prophecy will cease ***(1 Cor. 13:8)***.

a. **Solution One-** Miracles were prominent during the era of Moses, Elijah, Elisha, and as well as Jesus and His apostles, but these are not the only occurrences found throughout the Bible. God visited Abraham face to face ***(Gen. 18; 21-22)***, Samson had supernatural strength imparted by the Lord ***(Jud. 15:1-20)***, and the list continues. There are more than 83 supernatural miracles recorded in the Old Testament alone. Now, some may point to the dispensation they were living in, but the argument that gifts decreased at the turn of the first century is an invalid argument. During the church age called the "Dark Ages," "Justification by Faith" was a foreign concept, but it does not mean that this doctrinal truth was invalid.

There is evidence that the gifts of the Spirit have been in operation for the last two thousand years. Early church leaders recorded miracles such as: Justin Martyr (100-165 A.D.) recorded that the prophetic gifts remained with them in his *Dialogue With Trypho*; Irenaeus (130-202 AD) testified of men being raised from the dead; Tertullian (160-240 AD) held to the belief that the same apostolic power that rested on Paul was also with them; Origen (185-253 AD) noted believers received the Holy Spirit and cast out demons, cured the sick, and prophesied. Augustine of Hippo (354-430 AD) was a skeptic until a miracle occurred while he was at Milan, a blind man received his sight, and then at Hippo over 70 miracles were documented; Benedict of Nursia (480-547 A.D.) was known to raise the dead, heal the sick, and operate in the prophetic; Augustine of Canterbury (early 6th century-604 A.D.) was sent to Great Britian to spread the Gospel by Pope Gregory and as noted in history miracles accompanied his ministry; Ansgar (800-865 A.D.); Hildegard of Bingen (1098-1179 A.D.) was a leader of a Benedictine convent near Bingen and was known to speak and sing in tongues with Pope Eugenius III visiting her and after investigation, validated her claims of miracles; Francis of Assisi (1181-1226 A.D.) had miracles attributed to his ministry such as healing a paralytic; Vincent of Ferrier (1350-1419 A.D.) spoke in tongues and as he ministered to different ethnic groups, they recorded he would speak in their native tongue through the power of the Holy Spirit; Pilgram Marpeck (1495-1556 A.D.) defends the miraculous continuation and cites martyrs being raised from the dead; George Fox (1624-1691 A.D.) records miracles such as healing John Fox, a fellow Quaker, along with charismatic gifts in operation in his *Journal* and *Books of*

Miracles; Count Zinzendorf (1700-1760 A.D.) while seeking the Lord in 1727, during a prayer meeting, the Lord visited and supernatural healings took place with cancer being cured along with prophetic utterances given; John Wesley (1703-1791 A.D.) recorded numerous times of the Lord healing him as well during revival meetings having men and women "falling to the floor" underneath the power of God, laughing uncontrollably (even occurring to himself and his brother, Charles Wesley); Edward Irving (1792-1834 A.D.) sought the Lord for the supernatural and on April 31st, 1831, members from his church began to speak in tongues; Charles Parham (1873-1929 A.D.) had a watchnight service January 1st, 1901, with the students seeking the evidence of the Holy Ghost Baptism and within three days cloven tongues of fire rested on the heads of these students as they spoke in tongues. This list is not exhaustive, but it contains accounts that the miraculous never ceased. One cannot believe in divine healing and reject speaking in tongues; neither can it be dismissed due to "historical absence" being debunked. By these historical accounts, the supernatural gifts of the Spirit did not subside.

b. **Solution Two**- ***Acts 28:8-9*** is clear that as Paul was nearing the end of his ministry that he healed Publius' father on the island of Malta and all the diseased that came to him. Furthermore, the epistles were written for specific purposes, none of them are the same, but it does not mean we can dismiss the doctrine that is found in them. ***Galatians, James,*** and ***1 and 2 Thessalonians*** were written BEFORE ***1 Corinthians*** and mentions nothing about spiritual gifts.

c. **Solution Three**- Paul wrote ***1 Corinthians*** around 57 A.D.; the theory that they have proposed is the gift of healing subsided due to Paul not being able to heal himself from the thorn in his flesh recorded in ***2 Corinthians 12. 2 Corinthians*** was written around the same time, between 57-58 A.D.. How would the gifts begin ceasing within a year? What they refuse to take note of is that when Paul referenced the thorn in his flesh, he was referring to an incident that occurred 14 years prior ***(2 Cor. 12:2)***, meaning it would have been about 43-44 AD. How could the gifts pass away in 43-44 A.D. and then reappear for one letter to the church at Corinth in 57 A.D. and less than a year later God suspends the supernatural activity? The answer is simple…the gifts did not cease.

d. **Solution Four**- God has used signs to verify His power and position as King of kings and Lord of lords. When Elijah, in ***1 Kings 17-18***, prophesied that a drought would occur, God shut the heavens for three and a half years. Next, God used Elijah to pray down fire from Heaven to consume the sacrifice on the rebuilt altar. Jesus performed miracles and God did it to validate His Sonship ***(Acts 2:22);*** yet there is more. Miracles are three-fold: signs (validation of the message and messenger ***Mk. 16:20***), wonders (demonstration of God's omnipotence ***Ps. 19:1-4***), and gifts (edification of the body of Christ ***1 Cor. 12:7***).

e. **Solution Five**- ***Acts 2*** specifically says that the 120 disciples spoke in tongues, witnessing to at least 15 different ethnic groups declaring the wonderful works of God ***(Acts 2:11)***. However, this was a one-time event, every other time in ***Acts*** where tongues were recorded, the people spoke the same language as each other and it never said they understood one another *(**Acts 10**-* Cornelius' house; ***Acts 19***- 12 Ephesian believers*)*. There is not any doctrinal truth that solidifies this teaching because Paul said, *"For he that speaketh in an unknown tongue speaketh not unto men, but unto God: for no man understandeth him; howbeit in the Spirit he speaketh mysteries"* ***(1 Cor. 14:2)***. Something else to consider, Peter on the Day of Pentecost preached to the crowd; what language did Peter speak? Did he declare the prophetic utterance that Joel recorded in the Hebrew tongue? Greek? Hellenism spread and Greek became the common language. God did not need each person to speak in the various languages to speak the Gospel, it was used to CONFIRM the Gospel.

f. **Solution 6**- *"Charity never faileth: but whether there be prophecies, they shall fail; whether there be tongues, they shall cease; whether there be knowledge, it shall vanish away. [9] For we know in part, and we prophesy in part. [10] But when that which is perfect is come, then that which is in part shall be done away"* ***(1 Cor. 13:8-10)***. Tongues and prophecy WILL cease, when that which is perfect has come. This refers to the New Jerusalem, *"And I John saw the holy city, New Jerusalem, coming down from God out of Heaven, prepared as a bride adorned for her husband. [3] And I heard a great voice out of Heaven saying, Behold, the tabernacle of God is with men, and He will dwell with them, and* *they shall be His people, and God Himself shall be with them, and be their God. [4] And God shall wipe away all tears from their eyes; and there shall be no more death, neither sorrow, nor crying, neither shall there be any more pain: for the former things are passed away"* ***(Rev. 21:2-4)***. Exegeting the text, Paul was speaking about the glorious Return of Jesus Christ, His Second Advent and when after the thousand-year reign has ended, Satan will be loosed for a season and then utterly destroyed by being thrown into the eternal Lake of Fire as Jesus establishes an eternal Kingdom.

Testimony: My wife and I have pastored at Patrick Springs Pentecostal Holiness Church for the last two years. In a little over two years, we have had over 96 baptized in the Holy Ghost, evidenced by speaking in other tongues. We had a revival in Fall of 2023 and one of our sister churches came to support the meeting. One of the gentlemen from Christian View PH Church came to the altar seeking the Holy Ghost Baptism. I remember, Pastor Timothy Nail prayed on the left side, and I was on the right. As I laid hands on this older man, he was slain in the Spirit. Now, if you are reading this, you might poke fun because of the term "slain." Some do not believe that men and women, underneath the power of God, fall in the floor. I remind these skeptics that whenever the glory of God rested in the temple that Solomon had built *"the priests could not stand to minister by reason of the cloud" (2 Chron. 5:14).* One preacher declared, "Their knees buckled underneath the splendor of God's shekinah glory." There are plenteous examples that testified of men and women's encounters with God and His Spirit that left them lying on the ground or in a state of complete awe at His glory *(*c.f. *Matt. 17:5-6; 1 Kgs. 8:11; Dan. 8:15-18; Exod. 33:10; 40:34-35).*

Chapter 3

Church's Conflict

For he that speaketh in an unknown tongue speaketh not unto men, but unto God: for no man understandeth him; howbeit in the Spirit he speaketh mysteries ***(1 Cor. 14:2).***

This Scripture has been used numerous times, but it cannot be overemphasized enough due to the context. Paul is stating that when one speaks in tongues, they are speaking in mysteries. As Pentecostals, we believe in a prayer language. Here lies the second issue where there are those who believe in the gifts of the Spirit but are hard pressed that if someone speaks in tongues there MUST be an interpreter. But is this true?

- **Example 1-** ***Acts 2*** does say that those in Jerusalem understood them, but this is the only case where this happened. Also, we must examine what Paul said in ***1 Corinthians 14:27*** *"If any man speak in an unknown tongue, let it be by two, or at the most by three, and that by course; and let* *one interpret."* Would Paul be contradicting the Holy Ghost? Absolutely NOT! ***Acts 10*** there was NO interpretation at Cornelius' house. Even Paul prayed over the Ephesian believers and simultaneously all 12 men spoke in tongues without any interpretation in ***Acts 19.*** What is the difference? As mentioned before, tongues were used as evidence, edification, and exaltation. Whenever one is baptized in the Holy Ghost, there needs no interpretation because it is the initial, physical evidence someone has received power. If I touched a stove top that was set too high, the evidence is usually a blister. In the same way, when one is touched by the Holy Ghost, endued with His presence and power, they WILL speak in tongues.

- **Example 2-** The apostle Paul said to the Corinthian believers, *"I would that ye all spake with tongues"* ***(I Cor. 14:5)***. Bishop B.E. Underwood commented on this verse and said, "This is not referring to the manifestation gift, but to tongues as a means of worship for the individual." Paul, to say he wished they all spoke in tongues, would be strange if he was not implying this is a universal gift for all believers. In ***verse 23*** he implies that they all do speak in tongues when he writes, 'If therefore the whole church should assemble together and all speak in tongues...' (NASB). This indicates that all of them were tongue-talkers. The whole context of ***1 Corinthians 14*** is based on this premise. Examining this chapter gives further insight to how tongues are used in the life of the New Testament Believer.

- **Example 3-** Paul mentions that he not only prays in the Spirit, but he sings in the Spirit as well ***(1 Cor. 14:15).*** Here, Paul illuminates the benefits for personal use of tongues. Praying in the Spirit comes from the individual's spirit, as well as singing in the Spirit, bypassing the intellect of man. Critics will attempt to sway this passage in favor of tongues only being useful with an interpretation, but this is most certainly not the case. Paul did not condone the rejection or forbiddance of speaking in tongues, but his heart's desire was to see the local assembly edified.

Praying and singing in the Spirit is a personal way a believer can be strengthened by the Holy Ghost. Dr. Ray H. Hughes said, "Paul allowed for praying and singing in tongues...When one speaks with tongues he gives thanks as well ***(v. 17).*** Paul followed this statement by a declaration, *'I thank my God, I speak in tongues more than ye all'* ***(v. 18).***" The apostle Paul was not referencing his ability to speak multiple languages, being multilingual; rather, he was testifying of his personal experience. Following this chapter, in ***verse 21***, he addressed the prophecy of Isaiah in ***Isaiah 28:11****: 'In the law it is written, With men of other tongues and other lips will I speak to this people."* The very next verse he describes tongues as being a sign to unbelievers.

The conclusion of ***chapter 14*** Paul is making certain that no one in the church forbade the operation of tongues. As the apostle admonished them, neither should we ever regulate the operation of the Holy Ghost in the church.

Testimony: My father, Rev. D.A. Leonard was in his early twenties when he conducted a revival in Old Fort, North Carolina. The church was Independent Baptist, and although they were boisterous in their worship, they did not believe nor allow anyone to speak in tongues. The pastor was battling aggressive throat cancer and was given a short time to live. As my father was preaching, he heard the Lord say, "If he will allow me to Baptize him in My Spirit, I will heal his throat cancer." Apprehensive but obedient, my father looked at the pastor and told him what the Lord had said. The pastor, with tears in his eyes and barely able to talk said, "I want to receive." As my father laid his hands on the pastor's head, it began with a painful whisper, then a strong voice – this Baptist pastor started speaking in tongues. Not only was he instantaneously filled with the Holy Ghost, but he was also healed of cancer by the power of God, continuing to pastor the church for many years.

Chapter 4- Personal Covenant

Then Peter said unto them, Repent, and be baptized every one of you in the Name of Jesus Christ for the remission of sins, and ye shall receive the gift of the Holy Ghost. [39] *For the promise is unto you, and to your children, and to all that are afar off, even as many as the Lord our God shall call"* ***(Acts 2:38-39)***.

After examining the use of tongues and solidifying the validity of this gift, this book would not be complete without informing the reader that the Holy Ghost desires to give each believer their personal Pentecost. The above text, Peter is preaching a specific message after the 120 were endued with power, and declared to those who were listening and desiring to be saved that if they would believe (appropriated faith in nothing more and nothing less than Christ's finished work on Calvary) and be water baptized (whether in Jesus Name or Father, Son, and Holy Ghost – this is an act of obedience), they would receive the gift of the Holy Ghost. The word "gift" that is used here is *dorean* and means "a gift (without repayment)." You nor I can deserve the Holy Ghost baptism, but every good and perfect gift comes directly and divinely from God ***(Jam. 1:17)***. Not only is this a gift, but a generational promise. The early Western church experienced Pentecost in the late 19th century into the early 20th century. Many have heard about Charles Parham and Topeka, Kansas, the Azusa Street revival with William J. Seymour and more. Within the last hundred years, the message of Pentecost has seemed to be forgotten with movements being localized; nevertheless, this promise is not invalid. There is a generational impartation the Holy Ghost is desiring to distribute to you and all who believe. For those who have not experienced this promise, I want to explain how one is able to be a viable vessel.

- **Forgiveness (salvation)-** You must be saved to have the Holy Ghost Baptism. If you are not saved, stop here and realize that Jesus Christ loves you and this whole world becoming the sacrificial Lamb. He was beaten, bruised, chastised and crucified for our sins. Nevertheless, death could not hold Him, the devil could not destroy Him, and our sin could not distance Him from us. ***Ephesians 2:8*** tells us, *"For by grace are ye saved through faith; and that not of yourselves: it is the gift of God."* To be saved, all it takes is to repent from your sins (turn away), placing your faith in

Christ and asking Him to be Lord over your life.

- **Faith (submission)-** Every gift from God must be accepted with faith. Scripture says Christ could not perform many miracles in Nazareth because of their unbelief ***(Matt. 13:58)***. If you doubt, you will do without; yet this is not God's will. He desires to bless YOU ***(Ps. 84:11)***. Faith is the avenue to God's favor because without it, no one can please God ***(Heb. 11:6)***; it is impossible to receive God's impartation without faith ***(Jam. 1:6)***.

- **Fervor (seeking)**- Have you ever heard the expression, "You can take a horse to water, but you cannot make him drink?" Many will feel the Spirit's power on them, but they have a closed mouth. Some will have stammering lips, which is a precursor to the Spirit Baptism, but they stop and grow disheartened. I have heard some say, "Well, I guess this gift is not for me." This is preposterous, the Holy Ghost Baptism is for ALL believers. The Baptism of the Holy Ghost is evidenced by SPEAKING in other tongues – this is not only **VISIBLE** but **VOCAL**. One will never receive the Holy Ghost Baptism with their mouth sealed. It is your mouth and your voice, but it is His utterance. Next, some will say, "Just say 'Hallelujah!'"

Now, I do not want to sound critical because God's presence rides on the wings of praise, but I propose this question: "Can you speak in Spanish and English at the same time?" The answer is, "No." Neither can one speak in tongues and English simultaneously. Enter God's presence through praise and as the Spirit of God is on you, open your mouth and speak, allowing the utterance to flow. Do not think of the way your words will sound, God is not filling you through intellectualism, but God bypasses the mind and fills you from the innermost, your belly ***(Jn. 7:38)***.

Conclusion

I close with this, as the Holy Ghost Baptism is described as a river of living water, Satan wishes to dam God's gift inside of you. There are three major hindrances to the Holy Ghost Baptism:

- **Unforgiveness**- Between the belly and mouth, there is an organ called the "heart." Now, this is not only referenced as an organ in the Bible, but it controls our emotions ***(Jer. 17:9; Ps. 73:26)***. Solomon records, *"Above all else, guard your heart, for everything you do flows from it"* **(Prov. 4:23 NIV)**. Christ took this offence so seriously that if one were to offer a sacrifice, knowing that their brother had an ought against them, they were to leave their sacrifice and allow reconciliation ***(Matt. 5:23)***. Christ also reiterated the penalty for unforgiveness by citing the Father would not forgive us if we do not forgive others ***(Matt. 6:15)***. The Lord desires to Baptize you in His Spirit, but the first item on His agenda is for your heart to be in harmony with His. I encourage you, if you are reading this and are experiencing this struggle – go to them, no matter what was said or done, be obedient to God. Obedience is the key to overflow.

- **Unbelief**- I used to hear this in many revivals as I was an adolescent, and mentioned this above, "If you doubt, you will do without, but if you believe you shall receive." James tells us, *"But let him ask in faith, nothing wavering. For he that wavereth is like a wave of the sea driven with the wind and tossed"* ***(Jam. 1:6)***. Every gift from God is dependent upon faith. For those who are sick and desire healing, we are directed to pray the prayer of **faith** ***(Jam. 5:13-16)***. Faith unlocks favor, do not allow any deceptive lie from the enemy to keep you from being empowered by the Spirit.

- **Unrepentant Sin**- Sin barricades God's blessings from our lives as noted in Scripture (***Isa. 59:2; Jn. 9:31***). If there is persistent sin, the Spirit Baptism will not be accessible. This does not mean one will not struggle with the flesh or battle. The Spirit Baptism is not for the perfect but the willing. Below is the testimony of how God will dynamite the spiritual dam for those who are willing to surrender sin in their life and seek for the higher power of Heaven.

Testimony: A lady in our church, with her permission to share the story, was desiring to receive the Holy Ghost Baptism. She was raised Primitive Baptist but had found herself in the Pentecostal church. I visited her father in the hospital whenever she began to share her heart's desire to receive this gift from God. She asked me, "Pastor, why does their seem to be a hindrance?" As mentioned in this book, I listed unforgiveness or doubt, but then I realized one more item – sin. Now, most would point out the "big sins," homosexuality, fornication, etc. However, she admitted that she liked to have a glass of wine. She was not a drunkard, never abused alcohol, but the Lord had been dealing with her about this. This book is not going to argue whether drinking is permissible or not, for we believe in the IPHC total abstinence; yet this lady yearned for the Lord. That Friday, as we had this conversation, I was unaware what would take place shortly after. That very day she purposed in her heart to totally surrender to the Lord; no more would even a social drink be allowed. That Sunday, two days later, without being prompted or pulled, without having someone "coach her," she ran to the altar and Christ Himself baptized her in the Holy Ghost. I asked her, not knowing what she had or had not done, "What changed?" She consecrated herself to the

Lord. What Christ did for her, I still believe He will do for you.

Bibliography

Beacham, A.D. Jr.. *Light for the Journey: A Fresh Focus on Doctrine.* Franklin Springs: LifeSprings Resources, 1998.

Brooks, Noel. *Charismatic Ministries in the New Testament.* Greenville: Holmes Memorial Church, 1988.

Horton, Stanley M.. *Acts: A Logion Press Commentary.* Springfield: Logion Press, 2014.

Hughes, Ray H.. *Who is the Holy Ghost: A Study of the Person and Work of the Holy Spirit.* Cleveland: Pathway Press, 2004.

Hyatt, Eddie L.. *2000 Years of Charismatic Christianity: A 21st Look at Church History from a Pentecostal/Charismatic Perspective.* Lake Mary: Charisma House, 2002.

Pike, Garnet E.. *Receiving the Promise of the Father: How to Be Baptized in the Holy Spirit.* Franklin Springs: LifeSprings Resources, 1997.

Synan, Vinson. *Old Time Power: A Centennial History of the International Pentecostal Holiness Church.* Franklin Springs: LifeSprings Resources, 1998.

Tramel, Terry. *The Beauty of the Balance: Toward an Evangelical-Pentecostal Theology.* Franklin Springs: LifeSprings Resources, 2009.

Tunstall, Frank. *Discovering the Job Description of the Holy Spirit.* Maitland: Xulon Press, 2020.

Underwood, B. E.. *Spiritual Gifts: Ministries and Manifestations.* Franklin Springs: LifeSprings Resources, 1984.

Made in the USA
Columbia, SC
14 May 2025